ANIMAL DETE[CTIVES]

DETECTIO[N RATS]

Rosie Albright

PowerKiDS press™
New York

Published in 2012 by The Rosen Publishing Group, Inc.
29 East 21st Street, New York, NY 10010

First Edition

Editor: Joanne Randolph
Book Design: Kate Laczynski

Library of Congress Cataloging-in-Publication Data

Albright, Rosie.
 Detection rats / by Rosie Albright. — 1st ed.
     p. cm. — (Animal detectives)
 Includes index.
 ISBN 978-1-4488-6149-1 (library binding) — ISBN 978-1-4488-6256-6 (pbk.) — ISBN 978-1-4488-6257-3 (6-pack)
 1. Sniffer rats—Juvenile literature. 2. Land mines—Detection—Juvenile literature. I. Title.
 SF459.R3A53 2012
 636.935'2—dc23

                                        2011022774

Manufactured in the United States of America

CPSIA Compliance Information: Batch #WW12PK: For Further Information contact Rosen Publishing, New York, New York at 1-800-237-9932

CONTENTS

Detection rats are trained to save lives.

Rats are smart and easy to train. They cost less to use than dogs do, too.

Most detection rats are
African pouched rats.
These are the largest rats
in the world.

African pouched rats have a great sense of smell. Wild rats use their noses to find food.

Trainers use food to train the rats. They teach the rats to sniff out **land mines**.

13

Land mines blow up if people touch them. Some countries have fields of land mines.

If a rat smells a land mine, it stops. Then it stands in a special way called pointing.

17

Rats can check a **mine field** much faster than people can.

Rats are trained to smell a deadly **lung** illness, too. Then people can get drugs to make them better.

Detection rats work mainly in Africa right now. Soon they could be used all over the world!

WORDS TO KNOW

land mine

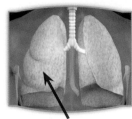

lung

mine field

INDEX

WEB SITES

Due to the changing nature of Internet links, PowerKids Press has developed an online list of Web sites related to the subject of this book. This site is updated regularly. Please use this link to access the list: www.powerkidslinks.com/andt/rats/